justice

and

Fair Play

THE INTERGOVERNMENTAL CONFERENCE OF THE EUROPEAN UNION

1996

Federal Trust Papers Number Six

THE FEDERAL TRUST

The Federal Trust was founded in 1945 to study the future of democratic unity between states and peoples. The principal focus of its work has been the European Union and the United Kingdom's role within it.

The Federal Trust conducts enquiries, promotes seminars and conferences and publishes on a wide range of contemporary issues — most recently (apart from the IGC) on pensions reform and on the European information society. Its current work programme includes a study of public-private partnerships in the European Union.

The Trust has also established a major European education programme for sixth forms, universities and young leaders. It is involved in several projects to enhance the European dimension in the curriculum.

The Federal Trust is the UK member of TEPSA (the Trans-European Policy Studies Association).

PUBLISHED BY THE FEDERAL TRUST
11 TUFTON STREET
LONDON SW1P 3QB

© FEDERAL TRUST FOR EDUCATION AND RESEARCH,
  APRIL 1996

ISBN 0 90157357 4
ISSN 1357 3314

Federal Trust Round Table

The European Union's Intergovernmental Conference opened in Turin on 29 March 1996. A Federal Trust Round Table has been established to discuss in depth the issues raised by the IGC, to monitor the processes of its preparation, negotiation and ratification, and, later, to assess its outcome.

The following **Federal Trust Papers** have appeared so far:

No. 1   *State of the Union*   February 1995
No. 2   *Towards the Single Currency*   May 1995
No. 3   *Building the Union: reform of the institutions*
            June 1995
No. 4   *Security of the Union*   October 1995
No. 5   *Enlarging the Union*   February 1996

The next, No. 7, *Prosperity of the Union*, will appear in July.

The Round Table is chaired by Lord Jenkins of Hillhead, President of the European Commission 1977-81; the rapporteur is John Pinder, Chairman of the Federal Trust; the secretary is Andrew Duff, Director of the Trust, to whom any written comments should be addressed.

The members of the Round Table, shown on the following page, serve in an independent capacity and do not represent their organisations. They do not necessarily concur with all the opinions expressed in this **Federal Trust Paper**, but they support its general thrust and welcome it as a contribution to the debate about the future of the Union.

The Federal Trust is an independent charity and, as such, holds no political view of its own.

The Trust acknowledges the support of the Nuffield Foundation for its continuing work on citizenship.

Members of the Federal Trust Round Table

Justice and Fair Play

The European Union (EU) has brought many benefits to those living within its borders, but for the great majority it still appears remote, secretive, mysterious and interfering. There are many things that can and should be done to remedy this state of affairs. In this Federal Trust Paper we consider how the rights of individual citizens could be extended and safeguarded, how more substance could be given to citizenship of the Union, and how human rights could be more effectively protected; our aims are to strengthen the rule of law, make the legislative processes more transparent and improve people's access to justice.

The job of the Intergovernmental Conference (IGC) that began in Turin on 29 March 1996 is to make the government of the European Union work better in the common interest of all Europeans. It has a heavy duty not just to the fifteen member states of the Union and their peoples but also towards those citizens of Europe as yet outside the Union and who aspire to join it. Much has been said and written on the subject by lawyers and students of European integration; it is high time for the debate to be broadened out to the public domain, for the debate over the future of Europe is now a democratic one, affecting us all. Three out of five European citizens are currently dissatisfied with the way democracy works in the European Union.[1] If the IGC is to deal capably with that problem, it will have to rise above institutional tinkering and recognise that what Europeans both expect and deserve of their government at all levels is justice and fair play.

THE EUROPEAN CITIZEN [2]

European citizenship: the story so far

The concept of citizenship of the European Union has a long pedigree. The Treaty of Rome (1957) talked of an 'ever closer union among the peoples of Europe'. The key idea that underpins the gradual development of popular legitimacy for European integration is enshrined in Article 6 of the Treaty which outlaws discrimination on the grounds of nationality. Over the years this objective of the European Community has begun to be realised, and 'European citizenship' has featured widely, at least as a rhetorical device.

The process of economic integration and legal harmonisation has gone hand in hand with the gradual democratisation of the common institutions. The outstanding development was the first election by universal suffrage of the European Parliament in 1979 — the only directly elected international parliament in history. Many, especially on the mainland, regard the Parliament as the sovereign body of the European citizen-elector, and European citizenship as the avant-garde of a federal union; others would be less excited by it; but all should hold it in respect because it does provide a direct link between the individual and the institutions, and is a source of democratic control.

In the 1980s efforts were made to stimulate the notion of 'a people's Europe', and several cultural projects, including the promotion of exchange between students and scholars, were launched by the Commission. Member state passports were given a common format and colour. More important, inevitably, was the wider public benefit of economic integration, and, in particular, the establishment of the ambitious programme to create a single market by the end of 1992 based on four freedoms of movement for goods, services, capital and also people. The combined effect of both European Community primary legislation and judgments of the European Court of Justice (ECJ) has been to make it possible for most people — workers, their families and students — to settle anywhere they like within the Union and to enjoy comparable social, economic and civic rights to natives.

Article 8 of the Treaty of Maastricht (1992) formally establishes citizenship of the Union for everyone holding the nationality of a member state. When the Treaty is fully implemented, EU citizens will enjoy rights and duties under the Treaty, which include the right to vote and stand in municipal and European Parliamentary elections wherever they live, to enjoy common diplomatic and consular protection, and the right to petition the European Parliament and to appeal to its new Ombudsman. The Treaty also enables the citizenship provisions to be developed by the Council acting unanimously on a proposal of the Commission (with the Parliament merely consulted). No action of this kind has yet been taken because the UK and to a lesser extent Denmark see European citizenship as a 'threat to national identity', and oppose its development.[3] The British government is worried that the creation of more EU citizens' rights would lead to reciprocal duties which are the preserve of states to impose, such as military service and taxation. 'The EU, however, is not a state, and should take care not to develop ideas which feed people's fear that it has a vocation to become one'.[4] We take the view, however, that a stronger commitment to common European citizenship will reinforce democracy and the rule of law and help the Union run better. And public opinion overwhelmingly expects the EU to play a leading part in fighting crime and in ensuring citizens' rights.[5]

In addition, Maastricht prescribed that the Community should be run according to the federalist principle of subsidiarity — in other words, that action can be taken at the European level in those many areas where the EU has shared competence with the member states only where there are implications for more than one member state, where the scale of action is proportionate to that of the problem and where the results achieved corporately will be better than those that would otherwise be achieved unilaterally.[6] Subsidiarity was, rightly, taken to imply a tendency to decentralisation — a view that was reinforced by the preamble which declared that decisions in the Union should be taken 'as close as possible to the citizen'.[7] It is an illusion to believe that transparency, accountability and respect for the rule of law in the administration of the Union can be achieved only by reforms, whether political or legal, at the centre. For this reason, in future, subsidiarity must be practised (as well as preached) not only in the regulatory field, but in the management and administration of the Union. The IGC is to consider whether or not to entrench in the Treaty the rules regarding the application of subsidiarity agreed at the Edinburgh European Council in December 1992.[8]

The problem is that subsidiarity is not about the allocation of competences, which is the job of the Treaty, but about how competences are to be exercised at every level of government — up, as well as down. Subsidiarity implies a far greater level of accountability at national and regional level. Since Maastricht, the Commission has been acting with considerable self-restraint, and has been affected by the closer association of some national parliaments in the scrutiny of Union institutions.[9] The newly created Committee of the Regions may also act in such a way as to surprise sceptics and to strengthen the links which exist between the centre and more peripheral regions of the Union.

Human rights

After Europe's descent into chaos during the first half of this century, it was the great achievement of the Council of Europe to have contributed to the guarantee and safeguard of civil liberty first in Western Europe and, latterly, one hopes, in Central and Eastern Europe. This has been the contribution of the European Convention for the Protection of Human Rights and Fundamental Freedoms (1950) and its later Protocols. Unlike citizenship of the European Union, the European Convention (ECHR) affects not just nationals of member states but all people, including foreigners, within its purview.

The ECHR is international law, under the jurisdiction of the European Court of Human Rights at Strasbourg, and therefore differs from EC law, whose arbiter, the Court of Justice at Luxembourg, has a federal supremacy over member state law. In so far as the EU member states are concerned, however, the two traditions of the Council of Europe and the European Community are closely associated, and the work of the ECJ has always been informed by the European Convention. Civil rights in Europe, therefore, have grown incrementally, with the EC and the Council of Europe working in parallel.[10] The main effect of the Council is to set human rights standards and to extend those rights to a wider category of people than nationals of EU member states; the main effect of the EU is to enforce the direct and uniform application of the rule of law in the matters where the EC has competence.

Neither jurisdiction, however, is without exceptions and derogations. For example, the EC's general employment rights do not apply to the civil services of the member states; freedom to own property under the terms of the ECHR is restricted by five EU member states; EC law on freedom to exercise a profession is impeded by restrictions in no less than eight member states; and so on.[11] Although there are moves towards agreeing a common visa policy with regard to third countries, the European Union itself is far from being a passport union. Examples of free travel areas within the Union are limited and imperfect — for example, between the UK and Ireland, and, now, within a hard core of the member states of the non-EU Schengen Agreement. Above all, each member state still has different rules about immigration and refugees. The right to acquire nationality and to be deprived of it firmly remains the unilateral decision of the individual states. Virtually the only civil duties which are fully portable between one member state and another are the obligation to obey the law and pay taxes.

In the IGC there will be a proposal for the European Union itself to sign up to the ECHR. This has a particular resonance in the UK and Ireland, where the Convention has not been incorporated into domestic law. This lapse stems from the initial nervousness of the post-war Labour government in agreeing to the Convention at all: Chancellor of the Exchequer Stafford Cripps feared that the ECHR would prevent his inspectors from entering people's homes in pursuit of the planned economy; Lord Chancellor Jowitt believed that the Convention would 'jeopardise our whole system of law' and upset senior judges.[12] There has been much debate ever since on the right-wing of politics about how to protect the

5

British state against its subjects — or, conversely, among liberals, about how to strengthen the rights of citizens to have redress from the authorities in cases of injustice without unreasonable cost or delay. Meanwhile, the number of cases brought against the British government in the Strasbourg Court exceeds that of any other member state of the Council of Europe, giving rise to frustration and embarassment. We believe that **it is important to have more effective judicial review within the UK for breaches of human rights. This could be achieved by the full incorporation of the ECHR into UK law.**

As far as the Union itself is concerned, the position with regard to human rights is obscure. Article B of the Treaty provides that one of the objectives of the Union is to 'strengthen the protection of the rights and interests of the nationals of its member states through the introduction of a citizenship of the Union'. Article F.1 of the Treaty of Maastricht commits the Union to respecting the 'national identities of its Member States, whose systems of government are founded on the principles of democracy'. Article F.2 says the Union shall respect fundamental rights as guaranteed by the ECHR and 'as they result from the constitutional traditions common to the Member States, as general principles of Community law'. Article F.3 says, encouragingly, that the EU shall 'provide itself with the means necessary to attain its objectives and carry through its policies'. But Article L debars the ECJ from formal jurisdiction in human rights. The implications of this bizarre state of affairs are that, while EU member state governments are subject to the regime of the ECHR, and while the Union itself — and presumably its institutions — are bound to respect fundamental rights, enforcement is weakened as a result of the unsatisfactory juxtaposition of the Luxembourg and Strasbourg Courts and by the fact that the ECHR itself for the moment remains outside the Community's legal order.

Despite all this, much highly relevant EC legislation now exists in the field of human rights, particularly concerning equal opportunities between men and women. EC law has a long reach: in November 1995 the ECJ ruled that the UK Prevention of

Terrorism Act contravened the 1964 EEC Directive on the treatment of foreign nationals.[13] The quantity and impact of such EC legislation will continue to grow, and we discuss below what might be done to improve the internal coherence of the Treaty on citizens' issues.

But the relationship between the Council of Europe, the European Community (which has legal personality), the European Union (which does not) and the member states is an unholy mess. In order to protect the interests of both EU citizens and foreigners who find themselves within the territory of the Union, it is surely desirable for the EC/EU to formalise and to strengthen its adherence to the ECHR. How precisely this should be done is troublesome. On 28 March 1996 the Court of Justice gave its opinion: accession could only be achieved by Treaty revision and not by Article 235; and whether or not the partners in the marriage would be compatible depended on the precise terms of the liaison. Thus the matter rests with the IGC. If formal accession is not possible, the intertwining of EC law with the ECHR should continue on a pragmatic case by case basis, whereby the ECJ continues to clarify the extent to which particular human rights form part of the general principles of EC law. But it might also be wise, in the context of enlargement, to write into the Treaty a penalty clause against a member state infringing human rights.

In the longer term, as the constitutional character of the European Union continues to mature, the case for a proper Bill of Rights becomes overwhelming. The European citizen needs to know how he or she is governed, by whom and from where. There have, indeed, been several proposals for a Charter of the European Citizen to be glued on to the Treaty.[14] Such a document would build on the ECHR and lay down standards of behaviour to which the EU institutions, its citizens and all member states should adhere. This would be a big step forward from Maastricht, however, and could transpire as part of a real settlement of the constitution of the Union — not, on the face of it, a realistic target for this IGC, but one it might set for its successor.

Cooperation in Justice and Home Affairs

The Treaty of Maastricht built into the Union a 'third pillar' to cover cooperation in the field of justice and interior affairs, in which the following are regarded as matters of 'common interest': asylum, immigration, drug trafficking, international fraud, judicial cooperation in both civil and criminal matters, and customs and police cooperation (Article K.1). These sensitive issues are dealt with behind closed doors by intergovernmental methods, and they largely evade both parliamentary scrutiny and judicial review.

The Maastricht IGC simply, if clumsily, transposed the procedures devised for the second pillar of Common Foreign and Security Policy (CFSP) across to the field of Cooperation in Justice and Home Affairs (CJHA).[15] This was a wholly inappropriate manoeuvre. CJHA is largely about the making of law; CFSP is mainly concerned with policy orientations and joint actions. That both tread into areas where traditional notions of 'national sovereignty' are pervasive implies neither that they need to be managed identically nor that they have to be ruled by minimalist consensus. In the case of the third pillar, at least there was some concession on the last point. A *passerelle* or footbridge was built so that the European Community (EC) institutions and single market procedures of the first pillar could on occasion be used in the field of asylum, immigration, drugs and fraud. But this facility, Article K.9 of the Treaty, can be exploited only by unanimous agreement of the member states. There is a similarly self-defeating provision for occasional use of the EC budget for CJHA purposes. Needless to add, neither opportunity has yet been grasped, and the interface of CJHA with the Community sphere continues to malfunction. Visa policy is a good example: the list of foreign countries whose nationals need a visa to enter the EU is laid down in an EC regulation (first pillar), but the conditions for their entry are subject to strict unanimity in the third pillar. Drugs policy is covered in the third pillar by Article K.1(4) (where Commission initiatives are possible), Article K.1(7, 8, 9) (where Commission initiatives are impossible), and in the first pillar by Article 129 (where co-decision applies); and we are blessed with the luxury of two drugs agencies, an EC Drugs Observatory in Lisbon and a Europol Drugs Unit.

The resulting decision-making structure is top-heavy, with a supplementary body of interior ministry officials — the intriguing 'K.4 Committee' — interposed between the Council's normal committee of permanent representatives, Coreper, and three lower level steering groups, who sit above as many as sixteen technical working parties. Output from this ponderous system relies almost wholly on the ability of an over-stressed Council presidency to hack the lowest common denominator of an agreement between mostly monoglot functionaries from the police, customs, and immigration services.

In the field of CJHA, the Maastricht IGC made no substantive changes to what had gone before — essentially ad hoc arrangements in the field of immigration and police cooperation — and has had, in the Commission's words, 'no significant innovative impact'.[16] None of the pre-Maastricht Conventions in the field of cross-border coordination — for example, *Ne bis in idem* (1987), transfer of convicts (1987), extradition (1989), prosecution (1990), asylum (1990) and sentencing (1991) — has yet come fully into force throughout the Union; and the record post-Maastricht has been equally lamentable. Even where Conventions can be implemented according to the Treaty by a two-thirds majority vote, the tyranny of consensus has still so far applied.[17] The only joint actions have concerned the drugs unit for Europol and travel facilities for children from third countries at school in the EU; and there have been about fifty non-binding Council resolutions, recommendations, reports, statements and 'conclusions'. Even the Group of Reflection was driven to conclude that in the third pillar the 'magnitude of the challenges is not matched by the results achieved so far in response to them'.[18] Only the UK government is sanguine about the achievements of the third pillar so far. 'Many specific agreements have been reached', it says — neglecting to add that none has been implemented.[19]

The vain presumption behind the third pillar was that it would be possible for member state governments to agree unanimously on the equitable sharing of burdens and on mutual reliance on one another's diverse regimes of law and order. Given the absence of the Commission to articulate a common interest and initiate proposals, and the lack of majority voting in the Council to induce a common decision, it is hardly surprising that this ambition has not been met. As expected, the desire for unanimity in everything is an effective source of paralysis.

Moreover, the exclusion of the European Parliament and the failure of member state parliaments means that CJHA is conducted beyond the dynamics of parliamentary scrutiny. Even the undertakings in the Treaty to consult MEPs from time to time have been neglected by member states: the Europol Convention was launched without notification of the Parliament. In 1995 a tough joint action on asylum, much criticised by the United Nations High Commission for Refugees, emerged from the K.4 Committee to the Council without any meaningful consultation of the European Parliament or of refugee bodies.[20] In our earlier Paper *Building the Union* we proposed the setting up of a joint committee of MPs and MEPs to monitor the work of the Council in the field of justice and home affairs.[21] We reiterate that proposal here, and urge that it be considered without waiting for the result of the IGC. Furthermore, as long as the third pillar remains intact, the right of assent to all legally-binding decisions that are not subject to a ratification process by national parliaments should be granted to the European Parliament.

The UK government is disparaging about the legitimacy of the European Parliament.[22] It also seems determined to oppose the extension of the role of the European Court of Justice to cover justice and home affairs. Here it stands alone. All its partners, the Commission and Parliament want the ECJ to guarantee the uniform interpretation of texts agreed under the third pillar. Most also believe it is necessary to improve the judicial scrutiny of intergovernmental action in sensitive areas that directly affect citizens' relations with each other and with the state authorities.

We agree. In addition, as we have seen, there are several areas where Community competence and third pillar matters overlap: free movement of persons, visas, customs, public health and fraud against the EC.

The establishment of Europol has been blocked by disagreement with Britain about judicial control; so also has closer cooperation between customs services, the introduction of common measures against corrupt officials, and a common policy on extradition and deportation. Despite the agreed common and growing threat of organised international crime — notably in the fields of drug trafficking, money laundering, terrorism, trade in radioactive materials and fraud in fine arts, antiques and stock exchange dealings — the UK government has set itself vehemently against the extension of the jurisdiction of the European Court of Justice into criminal law. Similarly, the British government is suspicious of EU measures to deepen action against racism and xenophobia;[23] and the Convention on the Crossing of External Borders is blocked by a legal dispute with Spain over Gibraltar.

We propose that the IGC amend Article L of the Treaty of Maastricht to extend the powers of the Court of Justice to cover human rights, justice and home affairs.[24] If the UK government were to block this reform, a derogation Protocol could be added to the Treaty committing its signatories alone to recognising the extension of the Court's jurisdiction in these areas.

In July 1995, chastened by the lack of progress under the third pillar — and stung by a Court action against it by the European Parliament for failure to act — the Commission proposed three directives whose purpose is to implement Article 7a of the Treaty in respect of the freedom of movement of persons. These proposals concern elimination of passport checks at the Union's internal frontiers, ease of passage for third country nationals lawfully resident in one member state to travel to another, and an improvement to two existing Directives on freedom of movement and establishment of workers and their families.[25] These proposals, which are dependent for their adoption on the coming into force of the blocked external frontiers Convention, are controversial, especially with the British government; but the choice of policy instrument — the EC Directive — is indubitably more appropriate than that of intergovernmental pacts. The large majority of the member states would wish the IGC to adopt a similar approach to the treatment of all related matters. This could be expedited relatively simply by the following reform measures:

- introduce qualified majority voting (QMV) for the use of the *passerelle* (Article K.9), and remove the need to have the decision ratified by member states;
- extend the scope of the *passerelle* to all Article K.1 matters;
- extend the Commission's right of initiative to all K.1 matters;
- replace conventions and joint actions with directives and regulations;
- enable the Commission to represent the Union on third pillar matters;
- unify expenditure under the EU budget;
- establish a timetable for the achievement of clear objectives.

Such a reform, leading to the general use of single market procedures on freedom of movement of people, would also have the effect of closing the gap between the treatment of EU citizens and the 12 - 14 million third country residents. Germany, in particular, is pushing for the transfer of asylum and immigration policy into Community competence — a reform we would strongly support — leading to a common status for and decent treatment of all third country nationals lawfully resident in the Union. As a first step, the process of communitarisation should begin in those areas where there are already major EC competences such as external border controls, customs cooperation and drug addiction.

For those items remaining in the third pillar, principally in the field of policing and criminal law, we hope it will be possible for the member states to agree that all Conventions should come into force once they have been ratified by only two-thirds of the member states. But Conventions will always be a highly unsatisfactory way for the member states of the Union to do business if they continue thereby to defy parliamentary scrutiny. If the UK succeeds in forcing the Union to retain the third pillar Conventions procedure, the IGC must agree to involve the European Parliament jointly with national parliaments in their scrutiny, even if on a confidential basis. Some thought should also be given to allowing Conventions adopted by fewer than the fifteen member states, approved by both national and European Parliaments, to have the status of EC law.

In short, the Union's treatment of Justice and Home Affairs requires of the IGC both new policy instruments and recast policy objectives, more democracy and transparency, a proper financing mechanism and a multi-annual work programme. Happily, this agenda is that of several governments, who also acknowledge that there is a very strong case for bringing the whole third pillar under the auspices of the European Community institutions.[26] Indeed, given the obvious shortcomings of CJHA and the close involvement of the Commission in the same field, the question inevitably arises about why we really need a separate pillar of the Union to deal with these citizens' matters. We can find no convincing answer to this question.

Schengen

Nevertheless, the complete dismantling of the third pillar cannot be accomplished until the Schengen Agreement, which foreshadows CJHA, is also integrated within the Treaty. Schengen is an unsatisfactory compromise, only partially operational, which might end up pleasing nobody but dividing the Union. It was conceived out of the frustration of the original members of the Community with the UK's obduracy about the abolition of internal frontier controls, and was always envisaged as a pathfinder to an EU-wide frontier free zone. The Schengen Treaty was signed in 1985 between Germany, France and Benelux, but it took five years before its practical implications were digested. Involving the exchange of police intelligence and the right to pursue suspects across national borders, Schengen has had a difficult and protracted birth. There are four reasons for this: first, problems with the SIS computer system required for data exchange; second, the lack of enthusiasm for the Agreement among those like the Dutch most concerned with transparency and democratic accountability; third, the bureaucratic weaknesses of the southern member states; and fourth, rising panic in France about immigration and drugs. But the fact that all member states apart from the UK have seen fit to deepen their cooperation outside the EU Treaty is damaging to the integrity of the Union and further isolates Britain.[27] Schengen effectively duplicates the objectives of the Treaty (Article 7a) with respect to the removal of the internal borders of the EU. **The Schengen Agreement can easily be transposed into Community law and, in our view, should be**. However, if the UK blocks this, the IGC should add a protocol to the Treaty on European Union to extend the jurisdiction of the ECJ to cover Schengen. Here, as in other matters, most of Britain's partners, including France, show a clear resolve to go forward on their own.[28]

The racial dimension

Acute concern about an influx of refugees from the Maghreb and from Eastern Europe, and its effect on unemployment, underlies much of the debate about Schengen and the third pillar. This anxiety is certainly exaggerated, however: official estimates suggest that only 3% of the total EU population are lawful immigrants, most of whom are Turks (2.5 m), ex-Yugoslavs and Moroccans (1 m each). After a flurry following the fall of Communism, primary immigration into the EU has almost stopped, with the exception of ethnic Germans and Greeks from East Europe and the Caucasus.[29] Nobody truly knows how many illegal immigrants there are in the Union, and estimates vary wildly. But applications for asylum to the EU fell from a peak of 693,000 in 1992 to 319,000 in 1994 after tough national restrictions were introduced during 1993. Those who fear that a common refugee policy of the EU would be in some way lax or permissive could not be more wrong: the danger is that it would be excessively restrictive and bordering on the inhumane.[30]

Much of the public fear of immigration is racial prejudice. The EU institutions have been rightly concerned with the growing evidence of racism and xenophobia within the EU since the decay and later dismemberment of the Soviet Union. At the instigation of the European Parliament, a Joint Declaration on Racism and Xenophobia was agreed in 1986, though this has an uncertain legal status.[31] The European Migrants Forum was set up in 1991, and proposals are now being made to toughen up anti-racist legislation, including the involvement of Europol in combatting racism and the inclusion of anti-discrimination clauses in all EC legislation. In the light, especially, of the forthcoming enlargement, it would also be desirable, in our view, for the IGC to **include the elimination of ethnic and religious discrimination as one of the main activities of the Union (Article 3)**.

The imminent further enlargement of the Union accentuates the importance of this proposal. Since the Treaty of Versailles, millions of Central and East Europeans have been living uncertainly as ethnic minorities in 'nation states'. EU enlargement is the chance to redress the balance against the essentially illiberal doctrine of the 'self-determination' of states.

The social dimension

The social dimension of EU citizenship is more widely accepted than its civil aspects, not least because the Commission has the general task of promoting cooperation in the social field.[32] Over the years, a number of important essential standards have been set down in EC directives to advance gender equality and to protect across the Union the health and safety of workers and their dependants. It was argued by some that in the single market programme flanking measures were needed to prevent 'social dumping'.[33] Latterly, however, the tendency towards liberalisation and competition in the European economies, combined with demographic trends, has led to measures designed to ensure labour market flexibility. It is now clear that the 'cradle to grave' welfare state with which Western Europe has been comfortably familiar since about 1950 will not be replicated at the level of the European Union. The emphasis has switched away from conventional social policy at both EU and national levels towards a new welfare settlement involving a better balance between the private and public sectors. The forthcoming transition to Stage Three of Economic and Monetary Union forces member state governments to tackle structural unemployment at home and to prepare national industry for the rigours of European and global competition. EMU also requires under-developed and peripheral regions of the Union to use to the full their comparative advantage in terms of unit labour costs. As mobility of labour throughout the Union is a relatively insignificant factor, there is unlikely to be much significant concerted pressure for the abolition of wage differentials within the EU.[34]

Nevertheless, the UK's partners will persist in their attempt to persuade it to surrender its derogation on the Social Chapter of the Treaty of Maastricht, whose adoption, they argue, would promote in Britain as elsewhere improvement of working conditions, a better informed workforce, and equality of opportunity between men and women. A change of government in Britain is more likely to resolve this issue than a change of heart by the Conservative Party. It is to be hoped that before long the regulatory framework will be put in place, financial services will be fully liberalised and minimum social standards will be agreed to enable the European citizen of the future to settle wherever he or she wishes in the Union with a truly portable job, pension, health and social insurance and even mortgage.

The addition, as we propose, of a racial to the gender criterion of the Treaty would change the character of the EU's social policy. Specific common measures in favour of the integration of ethnic minorities would emerge. Similar policies in favour of the integration of resident foreigners would also help to combat xenophobia.

What next for the European citizen?

If the IGC does not promise much immediately in terms of the social rights of citizenship, the omens are more promising in terms of civil rights. Unless there can be progress in developing quickly the civil society of the European Union, the skeletal European citizen of Maastricht might well remain as a ghost in the cupboard to haunt us. What are the ways to put flesh on the bones?

1.   Citizens have numerous rights that stem from the Treaties and from judgments of the ECJ, but they remain mostly ignorant of them. All the institutions have made progress in recent years in improving what is called their transparency. Even the Council has managed to adopt an admittedly cautious Code of Conduct on the publication of its proceedings.[35] Now adhesion to the principle of open government could be written into the Treaty. The single most important reform, as we suggested in *Building the Union*, is that **the Council should act in public when it debates and votes on EC law, and publish all drafts and working documents, as well as relevant minutes with all the texts agreed**. It is also desirable to **write into the Treaty a new Article 8f — the twin rights of access to public information and protection of private data**. A more ambitious proposal has been put forward that the Council should always meet in public unless it chooses to meet confidentially, and is able to justify the exceptions under the co-decision procedure.[36] The Commission and the European Parliament need to lead by example and up-grade the efficiency and probity of their administrations to the highest standards in the Union, namely those of Scandinavia. And to make its own contribution to the process of transparency, the IGC should progress the simplification and codification of EC law and consolidation of the Treaties in preparation for the final constitutional settlement of the Union (to coincide, amongst other things, with the expiry of the ECSC Treaty in 2002).

2.   As we have suggested above, the IGC is unlikely to go far to satisfy the proposals of the Spanish government and the European Parliament, among others, to write into the Treaty at

this stage a Charter of the European Citizen or Bill of Rights. That is likely to remain a project for this IGC's successor and for the EU institutions themselves whose role in the constituent process of the Union is at present attenuated, and needs to grow. For example, policies to give effect to new citizens' rights for non-discrimination in the fields of race, religion, gender, sexual orientation, disability and age should emerge through the normal political dialogue of the Brussels-based institutions and not *ex cathedra* from the IGC. But **the IGC should establish the legal base for such political development by adding these categories to that of nationality in Article 6**.

3.   The IGC has an honourable role to play, too, in helping the citizen-elector to contribute to and benefit from a deepening of the political system of the Union. The Round Table, among many others, has suggested that **electoral reform of the European Parliament** is a crucial next step in building popular legitimation for the Union — especially if the uniform electoral procedure has a strong regional foundation at the bottom and some supranational, EU-level list at the top. This, we argue, would encourage the development of genuine European political parties with the ability to articulate the anxieties and aspirations of the European citizen.[37] For the first time the Commission has joined the Parliament in calling for the IGC to progress the matter of the reform of Article 138(3).[38]

4.   The **powers of the Ombudsman** should be strengthened in three directions: first, to allow him to take EU institutions to the ECJ; second, to extend his competence to maladministration of EU policies within member states; and third, to cover third pillar Conventions.

5.   A growing number of people in Britain and elsewhere are either zealous for or resigned to **more referenda**, either at the national or at the EU level, in order to legitimate constitutional reform of the Union or to sanction the single currency. Others have suggested that the next President of the Commission — or a super president of the Council — should be directly elected by universal suffrage. Direct democracy is likely to be a greater

feature of EU politics than it has been to date, involving new and sophisticated methods of campaigning.

6.   Pressure for **decentralisation** within the Union, especially inside the big, old, centralised states, continues to grow and should, therefore, be encouraged to do so firmly within the perspective of the European dimension — especially in places, such as Northern Ireland and Gibraltar, where national citizenship is contested. The method of appointment of the Committee of the Regions should be changed to elevate the autonomous role of regional and local authorities. And the Union should sign up to the Council of Europe's Charter of Local Self-Government (1985) — and implement it.[39]

7.   The European Commission itself appears to place more emphasis on communication, education and culture as fruitful areas for the development of European citizenship. The birth of the **information society** in Europe, indeed, raises many questions about the role of the citizen in the European public space. Contemporary Europe will be a knowledge-based political society, with access to information, distance learning and entertainment of such a vast scope that it is difficult to envisage and encapsulate. The information technology revolution will transform the way our children learn, shop, receive services such as healthcare, enjoy themselves, and do their business and politics. The medium of the broadband superhighway will change the way people regard themselves and communicate with one other.[40] Already, the relatively old-fashioned and slow Internet has created a new, global and interdependent community of 'cyberspace' — certainly very different from Athens in 4th Century BC, but a real community nevertheless.

8.   The Maastricht Treaty opened up an **enhanced role for the Community in education**, although responsibility for the teaching curriculum remains with member state governments.[41] The Commission has taken a firm lead in promoting collaboration between schools and universities across the Union, and such exchange is bound to engender a sense of common European citizenship between many of those who experience it. Likewise,

the Union has since Maastricht a responsibility to support the common cultural heritage of the member states. Governments should lead where the Commission and much of the teaching profession wish to follow by fully recognising their own commitment to developing the European dimension in education. Sadly, this is not the case to date, especially in Britain.[42]

9.   There has been a useful and bold proposal for the establishment of a voluntary *Service Civique Européen* for young people — a **European 'peace corps'** — that is finding some support among member state governments. This could be an option in place of compulsory military service, already on the way out in France, enabling young people to work in multinational teams for popular causes such as cleaning up the environment, social services, cultural activities and humanitarian assistance both in and beyond the Union. A pilot scheme begins in 1996, and should be endorsed by the IGC.

THE EUROPEAN LEGAL ORDER
AT A CROSSROADS [43]

The IGC is faced with the challenge of how to reform the EU and EC Treaties so that the Union operates henceforth within a constitutional framework which is recognisable to its citizens and to the outside world. Minimum reforms should include clearing up the confusion between the European Union and Community, strengthening the role of the ECHR in Union law, widening the scope of judicial review of the administration or executive actions of the EU institutions, and streamlining and making more accessible to the citizen the administration of justice at the Union level. The pretensions of Maastricht in relation to citizenship, judicial and interior affairs have elevated public expectation of what 'Europe' might deliver; and crucial rulings of the ECJ in the last few years have encouraged citizens and companies to believe that Community jurisdiction can offer effective remedies for breaches of law. But there is still much to be done before the legal order offers the safeguards and protection that European citizens are entitled to expect now — let alone in a federal union.[44]

On the eve of the Union's further enlargement, its legal order stands at a crossroads. Without radical reform, the present system will remain a curious mix of supranational and intergovernmental, and will be limited at best to a 'constitutional order of states'.[45] Citizens' rights will not improve by magic or entirely by the inventive law-making of the European Courts.[46] In this section we examine some of the deficiencies of the present system and suggest reforms (not all of which require Treaty amendment), especially from the standpoint of the citizen-elector.

The rule of law

The rule of law is widely accepted as a fundamental requirement of any modern system of democratic government. The proposition that the European Union should be based on the rule of law is hardly open to serious contention; not only do its member states aspire to uphold 'the principles of liberty, democracy, and respect for human rights and fundamental freedoms and the rule of law', according to the preamble of the Treaty on European Union, but the European Community, centrepiece of the Union, is founded on respect for the rule of law.

The European Court of Justice, in its first opinion on the European Economic Area Agreement, confirmed that the Treaty 'constitutes the constitutional charter of a Community based on the rule of law'.[47] The Court's recognition of the constitutional nature of the Treaties reflects the gradual transition in the process of European integration, which has been evolving over some forty years, from customs union, to common market, economic and monetary union and a form of political union. The Court itself has not only made full use of its powers under the Treaty to promote the economic goals in the Treaties, but, in particular over the last decade, has endeavoured to ensure that the institutions pay proper respect to the rule of law in their law-making activities and that the benefits of Community law are made available to the European citizen.

It is perhaps in this latter respect that there have recently been the most remarkable judicial developments of the law since the ECJ's early rulings on the supremacy and direct effect in cases such as *Van Gend en Loos* (1962) and *Costa v. ENEL* (1964). In rulings such as *Francovich* (1991), *Factortame* (1996), *Brasseries de Pêcheur* and *British Telecom* (1996), the Court has developed the concept of direct effect to embrace secondary legislation as well as certain Treaty provisions. It has broadened, within the limitations imposed by the Treaty, the concept of 'direct and individual concern' to embrace a broader range of individuals, companies and other private sector bodies who may contest the validity of acts of the institutions before the European Courts and, crucially for those whose economic interests are damaged by a serious infringement of Community law, has established a right to damages.

Despite these encouraging developments in Community law, there are no grounds for complacency. The danger is that, at the IGC, member states will once again agree on an agenda which concentrates on the institutional preoccupations of states and their representatives rather than showing genuine concern for the citizen in his and her relationship with the Union. The fight to get a decent role for the European Parliament on the fringes of the IGC speaks volumes in this regard.

States' rights

The allocation of power within the Union (or 'competence' in the legal sense) between different levels of government — municipal, regional, national or European — is everywhere a sensitive political issue, and especially so in the three federal member states, Austria, Belgium and Germany.[48] To this extent, the argument over whether Article 3b on subsidiarity is justiciable is irrelevant: where a political solution is not forthcoming there must be a judicial settlement.[49] A more important issue is whether competence and jurisdiction should be allocated in binding legal terms to the EU with residual powers to the states — a problematical notion at a time when decentralisation and regionalism are in vogue — or whether certain entrenched powers should be reserved inalienably to the states, with the Union acting on the basis of delegated powers.

For over forty years, the EC institutions, especially the ECJ, have interpreted the Treaties functionally or teleologically in order to give maximum effect to the Treaty's goals of economic integration. Unlike other international courts, the ECJ has not usually interpreted member states' obligations to impinge as little as possible on national sovereignty: indeed, rather the reverse.

Although it is easy to see the political attraction, for example in the UK, of drawing a line beyond which 'Europe' could not interfere in matters reserved exclusively to national sovereignty, experience shows that almost all aspects of our national life today are potentially areas where some types of action may be more effective at international level. Health, culture, energy, education, crime, tourism, the harmonisation of private law, and environmental protection are all areas where regulatory activity takes place primarily at a national or even regional level. Yet all have a significant international and EU dimension. Even sport and leisure may have sufficient international character to warrant at least the application of horizontal EU rules of competition policy or free movement of workers. In addition, the increasing irrelevance of state frontiers in the field of information technology suggests that the allocation of responsibilities between different levels of government can only be handled on a pragmatic basis and should be subject to judicial control.

Legally, competence to act in particular areas of policy may be exclusively reserved to the EU institutions, or exclusive to the member state governments, or shared between them. Competence also involves settling the allocation of legislative or executive power between different EU institutions. In the last ten years, the European Parliament in particular has fought a number of battles in the ECJ in order to assert to the full its constitutional position in the law-making process.[50]

Finally, there remains the crucial issue of the competence of the Community or the Union to act in external relations. The lack of a clear image or 'personality' for the EC in international affairs significantly diminishes the credibility of Europe in world affairs.

In its *ERTA* judgement in 1971, the ECJ held that member states transferred powers to the EC institutions in external relations, in addition to those powers transferred expressly by Treaty, to the extent that the relevant field of activity was 'occupied' by Community legislation. Since then, many, if not most, fields of national political, economic and social activity have been occupied at least partially by Community rules, although the extent of occupation is constantly changing. The concept of EC competence is therefore dynamic. The ECJ, in a number of significant rulings, has carefully defined the boundary between EC and national competence in international economic relations. In political terms, the trend towards exclusive competence, with the Commission acting as negotiator and manager of the EC international relations, has slowed considerably, with mixed competence now being the rule. The Union as such currently has no legal competence to act or to be represented internationally.

Given the current state of Community law as laid down by the ECJ, it is clear that the issue of external competence can only be settled by agreement at the IGC.[51] **To move towards greater effectiveness in international relations, the IGC must endow the Community and Union with a single name and international personality**. It should also acknowledge the dynamic nature of competence in international relations and agree on a common format for diplomatic representation.

Any solution along these lines might well be at the expense of the Commission and in favour of the Council presidency, its secretariat and even a 'Mr or Ms CFSP'. Nonetheless, the inextricable link between the internal and external policies of the Union in all three pillars, as well as the pressures of globalisation, may require that conventional wisdom on the distinction between trade policy under Article 113 on the one hand and other fields of international relations be reviewed. The need for a coherent representation of EU monetary policy after EMU is an additional incentive for the IGC to reach a political solution in this area.

Priorities for change in the legal order

The current absence of clarity about competence, subsidiarity, legal personality, fundamental rights, citizenship and the constitutional nature of the Union itself, reflects the present critical state of European integration. The IGC will help if it can decide on the level of political and economic integration at which Europe can best defend the interests of its citizens. The emerging legal order will be no more and no less than a reflection of the political will.

Although confined mainly to economic issues, the ECJ has become a constitutional court, providing a large measure of judicial control in an embryonic constitutional and legal order. In its present form, however, the Community's legal order suffers from a number of serious defects. These include:

- the cumbersome nature of the law-making process;
- the privileged position of member states and institutions compared with private parties under Community law;
- difficulties and anomalies in access to justice at Community level;
- loopholes in the uniform enforcement of Community law;
- inadequate judicial control of administrative discretion particularly in enforcement, trade and competition policy actions;
- the virtual exclusion of judicial control in areas covered by the third pillar.

Administration of justice

Currently, the enforcement of EC law depends on infringement proceedings being taken by the Commission as guardian of the Treaties under Article 169 and by actions by individuals and companies invoking EC rights and obligations in national courts, subject to the supervisory jurisdiction of the ECJ under Article 177. The imperfection of this system derives largely from the political or judicial discretion which exists under both Treaty articles. There is within the Community no enforceable obligation on any institution to secure respect for the law. Much is made by the over-loaded institutions in Brussels, of the need to decentralise law enforcement, for example by action in national courts and by national competition authorities enforcing EC competition law. Progress has already been made in this area, encouraged by recent ECJ rulings confirming individuals' rights of action under Community law in national courts. But the system as a whole is weakened by excessive administrative and judicial discretion.

Finally, there is also a great need for the simplification of secondary EC law. In 1993 the Council committed itself to the wording of legislation that is clear, simple, concise and unambiguous. The rights and obligations of those to whom the act is to apply should be clearly defined, and the legal basis of the act should be justifed in simple terms. It is difficult to judge if these exhortations have been followed in practice. Simplification, with consolidation, is also required for the Treaties themselves which have become difficult to read and construe, as a result of successive amendments.

These suggested reforms have one element in common: they all relate to the administration of justice and the better achievement of the rule of law in the EU. Despite recent criticisms, the ECJ, complemented over the last six years by the Court of First Instance (CFI) has, on the whole, acted effectively to uphold the law of the Community, even if large areas of Community decision-making are still imbued by excessive administrative discretion which tends to escape effective judicial review. It is true that many of the fundamental principles of Community law, especially the concepts of the supremacy and direct effect of Community law, are not explicitly set out in the Treaties and have been derived by the Court from principles laid down in the Treaties. On the other hand, it is significant that, with the exception of recent criticisms emanating from certain quarters in the UK, the integrationist approach of the Court has not provoked allegations that it has usurped the role allocated to it under the Treaties.

As a constitutional court, it is obvious that, on many occasions, the ECJ has been called upon to reach decisions with political implications. Two examples of such cases are those involving relations between the institutions, particularly the Parliament, and the delimitation of the EC's competence in external relations. A further instance was the advisory opinion given by the Court at the request of the Commission in 1993 on the compatibility of the draft EEA Agreement with the EC Treaty.

It is perhaps understandable, particularly in the UK where the system of binding precedent is well-established, that some lawyers have felt that the ECJ's rulings lack consistency. Charges of arbitrary changes of direction by the Court are however hard to sustain. As a result largely of UK influence, the Court now often refers to its previous decisions. Despite the acknowledged political dimension of the Court's role, there have been virtually no assertions that the Court is politically motivated. Lord Mackenzie-Stuart, the first UK judge on the Court, commented that:

> 'The Treaties are the supreme authority until changed by the member states. Only the member states can change the substantive content of the Treaties. The Court cannot and has never sought to do so. Someone, however, has to resolve ambiguities. Member states can do this by Treaty amendment. Otherwise Article 164 places this task on the Court. By and large the Court has fulfilled this duty well.'[52]

Article 164 gives the Court the general power to 'ensure that in the interpretation and application of this Treaty the law is observed'. EU institutions, member states and private parties are subject to its jurisdiction, in principle on an entirely equal footing. The jurisdiction of the Court comprises essentially:

- actions by the Commission against member states for breach of EC law (Article 170);
- actions by one member state against another for breach of EC law (Article 170);
- Commission actions to enforce ECJ rulings (Article 171);

- actions brought by institutions against each other, by member states against the institutions or by individuals or companies against the institutions, to review the legality of acts of the institutions (Article 173);
- actions by institutions, member states and individuals or companies for a declaration that an institution has, in breach of a particular Treaty obligation, failed to act (Article 175);
- rulings given at the request of national courts to clarify the interpretation or validity of rules of Community law (Article 177);
- actions for damages against the institutions (Articles 178 and 215).

It is important to recall that the jurisdiction of the ECJ is both administrative, in providing judicial review of action or inaction by the institutions, and substantive, in interpreting and applying Community law. In criticising the Court or in proposing reform, it is therefore important to distinguish:

- the administration of justice in the EC (for example the structure and procedure of the Courts, the relationship between national and Community courts, jurisdiction and access) and
- the way in which substantive rules are applied including issues such as judicial law-making, the political or constitutional nature of the ECJ's rulings and the Courts' willingness to control or review administrative discretion.

Ironically, discussions about the rule of law in the EU have in the past frequently pointed to the relative absence of judicial control particularly in areas where the Commission takes decisions on complex economic facts, such as dumping, competition or state aids. Another criticism has been that the Court is unduly conservative on issues of admissibility, thereby restricting the categories of litigants who can bring cases before the Court. Against this background, it is a relatively recent phenomenon to hear criticism of the judicial activism of the Court. Many would argue that the Court has acted in too legalistic a manner and without sufficient regard for ensuring real justice and fair play.

Moreover, the enforcement of Community law by national courts is now as important as enforcement by the EU institutions. Much of Community law is an intrinsic part of national law and applied as such by national courts and tribunals. Apart from the ECJ and CFI, there are no special courts in the member states for the administration of Community law. More recently, one particular illustration of the importance of Community law as part of national law has been the liability of states (usually in damages) to individuals or companies, for failure of the state or its agencies to respect Community law. Two recent and striking examples of this phenomenon in the UK are the *Factortame* and *BCCI* cases.[53] The British government's opposition to enhancing the role of the European Court of Justice astonishes its Union partners, for the same government prides itself on its support for democracy and the rule of law, and insists on more effective implementation of EC law by all member states. The UK now threatens further proposals for the IGC to reduce or eliminate altogether state liability for the incorrect transposition of a directive when the state in question had acted in good faith.

Access to justice

Although the ECJ is now accustomed to acting as a constitutional court, in particular as regards the resolution of institutional conflicts arising from the constitutional order of the Treaties, the Court can do little, as the Treaties are currently drafted, to eliminate discrimination between the different subjects of Community law. The institutions, member states and national courts making references under Article 177 of the EC Treaty have a privileged position in litigation before the ECJ. States and institutions also enjoy procedural rights going far beyond those available to private parties. This is true as regards actions to contest the validity of Community acts; it is also true as regards the right to be heard in cases before the Court. Member states and institutions have a right to intervene and to be heard in all cases before the Court. This is not the case for private parties.

In a constitutional order where all subjects of the law have equal rights under the law, it seems inequitable and wrong in principle that certain entities, the institutions and member states should have a privileged position as regards recourse to justice. The inequalities which exist between the institutions and national authorities on the one hand and the private sector on the other have already been clearly illustrated in the economic field. The gap is even wider in political matters, and goes to the heart of the democratic deficit from which the Union currently suffers.

The imperfection of the Community legal order in constitutional matters is illustrated by the procedural difficulties confronting a political party seeking to enforce provisions of EC law in the Court of Justice. In the case of *Liberal Democrats v. European Parliament* no final decision was in fact rendered by the Court. It is likely however that it would have declared the action by the Liberal Democrats inadmissible on the grounds that a national political party had no 'direct and individual concern' in the issue of the European Parliament making a proposal under Article 138 of the Treaty for a uniform electoral procedure across the Community. Such a decision would have been based on the letter of Articles 173 and 175 as previously applied in economic matters. But why should economic case-law be a barrier to ensuring that a just and equitable result was achieved in an eminently constitutional matter, in full respect for general principles of (national) constitutional law? Since the Court of Justice is not formally bound by its previous decisions, it could perfectly well have held that, in a constitutional legal order, justice requires that political parties and even individuals enjoy the necessary procedural possibilities to secure the enforcement and application of constitutional rules, including those on elections.

It is significant that in the case in question neither the Commission nor the Council intervened before the Court. Thus, a finding of inadmissibility by the Court of Justice would have left Article 138(3) of the Treaty practically unenforceable by judicial means.

Simply to state, as in Article 8.2, that citizens 'shall enjoy the rights conferred by this Treaty' when those rights effectively mean that, in terms of access to justice at Union level, individuals are second-class citizens, is not sufficient. The core of the problem is the set of articles (in particular Articles 173, 175 and 177) which confer jurisdiction on the Court of Justice and which endorse the privileged position of member states and institutions.

In essence, although natural and legal persons are given express rights under Articles 173 and 175 to bring actions to annul acts of Community institutions or to force them to take action, in practice these provisions have been tightly circumscribed, notably by the Court's definition of the concept of 'direct and individual concern'. Defenders of the present system might well argue that, so long as effective remedies are available under national law enabling natural and legal persons to secure rights conferred by Community or Union law, then there is no legal vacuum. It is certainly true that comparatively recent decisions of the Court of Justice in cases such as *Factortame*, *Francovich* and *French Salmon* underline a member state's obligations under EC law as applied in national courts. Thus, the ruling in Factortame was to the effect that national courts have an obligation under Community law to refuse to apply a national statute which is incompatible with EC law — a revolutionary concept in the United Kingdom given the historical background of Parliamentary sovereignty. The Francovich case held that individuals who suffer damage as a result of a failure by a member state properly to implement a directive are entitled to damages. Likewise, in French Salmon, the Court held that individuals who had suffered as a result of a state aid which had not been notified under Article 93(3) were equally entitled to damages at national level.

Widening scope of EC jurisdiction

Despite these rulings, it is still the case that, for the most part, the actions of the institutions of the Union are subject to judicial review as a result of action by individuals only in a very limited sense. Any constitutional reform in this field would need to strike a balance between fostering and facilitating recourse to justice at national level (which is indispensable for the smooth functioning of the bulk of the economic law of the Union) and ensuring that natural and legal persons have full rights of action against the Union institutions where this is appropriate. It is difficult to predict areas of EU activity which will impinge on individuals. Once upon a time, areas such as equal pay, pensions, retirement provision, sports, broadcasting, fisheries, telecommunications and energy distribution might well have been thought to be relevant only to national governments and institutions. The exponential increase in the regulatory and decision-making powers of the EU institutions in these fields means that this is no longer the case.

More seriously, as far as fundamental rights and freedoms of the individual are concerned (which go to the heart of the issue of whether or not the rule of law can be said genuinely to exist in the Union legal order), the increasing activities of the Union in the fields of justice and home affairs highlight the inadequacy of existing remedies available to individuals under Union law against the institutions. To the extent that issues such as asylum policy, immigration policy and actions in the field of criminal law are transferred to Community competence by virtue of Article K.9, the inadequacy of the current means of redress by individuals against Union institutions will be underlined.

Moreover, although issues of national and local government are today of more immediate significance for the general public, this may not always be the case. Much may depend on the extent to which the abolition of internal frontiers makes inevitable a closer union of public (especially criminal) and private law, as well as the extent to which external pressures or threats force the Union to develop more operational responsibilities, for example on procurement in the fields of security and defence.

In any event, given the comprehensive scope of the current Union Treaty and its possible consolidation in a future constitutional conference, it is vital for the underlying political support for the Union that genuine improvements be made in the openness and accountability of the institutions, as well as in the possibilities of judicial review of their action or inaction. The provisions in the Maastricht Treaty recognising the importance of political parties at European level as a factor for integration within the Union were a step in the right direction. So are the new facilities of petition and recourse to the Ombudsman. The commitment by the institutions to openness is refreshing, though still not self-evidently put into practice. Until citizens in the regions feel that they are relevant to the political processes of the Union, it cannot be argued that the rule of law is respected in the fullest sense.

Legal order is as much a question of political practice as of legal or constitutional theory. The problem goes beyond the necessary reforms of the jurisdiction of the ECJ and CFI. Much depends on the improvements to the administration of justice at national, as well as Community level. Here, the system of judicial cooperation which operates under Article 177 is vital, yet it rests partly on chance. The recent ruling in the *Bosman* case illustrates this. The Commission had been aware for almost twenty years that the transfer system operated by European football clubs was incompatible with EC rules on competition policy and the free movement of workers. Nonetheless, for political reasons, the Commission hesitated to act. Now, as a result of a case initiated in the Belgian Courts and referred to the ECJ under Article 177, the application of Community law to football has been clarified.

The role of the Commission

The Bosman case illustrates the haphazard nature of the enforcement of Community law which stems from the current institutional system. The Commission is generally recognised as the 'guardian of the Treaties', yet it has no obligation under Article 169 to take measures to enforce EC law against member states. Despite the apparently mandatory language of Article 169, in practice the Commission exercises considerable discretion on whether to initiate Article 169 proceedings at all and, if so, on the timing of individual steps in the procedure, including the reference to the ECJ. Likewise, although Article 177 actually requires national courts to refer cases to Luxembourg in certain circumstances, national judicial practice under Article 177 is patchy, and the unusual features of the way in which this provision functions in practice diminishes the effectiveness of the ECJ — compared with a federal supreme court operating on the basis of appellate jurisdiction — in establishing a body of case-law providing guidance for national courts across the Union.

Despite the availability of an appropriate Treaty provision, member states play virtually no part in ensuring the enforcement of EC law in other states. The power granted under Article 170 of the Treaty for one state to sue another for failure to fulfil an obligation under the Treaty has almost never been used. In practice therefore, the enforcement of Community law against member states is subject to the political discretion of the Commission or is left to individuals who can demonstrate that their economic loss was caused by the failure of a government to respect its obligation under Community law. The absence of a credible system of law enforcement, particularly in 'high profile' areas such as the single market or citizens' rights, affects the credibility of the Community itself, reduces the economic impact of the single market and diminishes the rule of law.

Faced with a burgeoning number of complaints about the poor or non-application of EC law, the Commission has advocated a policy of decentralisation of law enforcement, with a greater role for national courts and tribunals. Although there has been a sharp rise in the number of cases involving Community law in national courts (ironically, given political Euroscepticism, especially in the UK), it will take time for economic operators, legal advisers and judges throughout the Union to play their full role in securing the application of Community law.

Despite the efforts made by the Commission to secure more openness and transparency in its procedures, the existence of Community law and the machinery involved in its enforcement under Article 169 remain a mystery to most individuals and enterprises. Compared with the wealth of documentation on the single market or EU financing, explanatory materials on the way to secure the enforcement of EC law are almost non-existent.

The Commission may decide whether to initiate cases which come to its attention in other ways than by private sector complaint. Of increasing and welcome significance are complaints from MEPs.

Although most Article 169 cases are started by complaint by the private sector, complainants have no formal role in the conduct of the complex and protracted proceedings. Thus, 'due process' is by no means assured. Should the Commission, for political or economic reasons, decide not to pursue a complaint under Article 169, the complainant has no possibility of judicial review of such a decision. Article 175 in theory offers a possibility of litigation on the question of an alleged failure to act by the Council, Commission or Parliament. Although such actions are potentially open to individuals and companies as well as to member states and the EC institutions, such possibilities have been greatly circumscribed by the Court and never admitted in the case of Article 169 procedures.

One major problem in this as in other matters concerning the administration of the single market is the fact that the Commission's resources are inadequate to the size of the task. The 1995 enlargement has exacerbated this problem, particularly linguistically. That the Commission is apparently ready to take 'appropriate action' under Article 169 (including recourse to the provisions of Article 171 regarding the imposition of sanctions) is of small comfort to a beleaguered business during the two or three years which procedures under this Article normally take.

If the single market is to be made to work, individuals and firms need to know that there are adequate means of redress available if they need them. The Commission clearly hoped that the provisions in the Maastricht Treaty on judicial cooperation would provide a framework for it and member state governments to act more effectively together. It is far from clear that the present system is producing results. Given the current backlog of work on Article 169 infringements, the prospect of further EU enlargement is distinctly worrying. The Commission needs more resources to cope.

Another major defect in the present Community legal order which has an adverse impact on the private sector is the mandatory use of the Directive as an instrument for EC legislation to build the single market. In this respect, there is an antithesis between the need for clarity and uniformity of EC law and the commitment to subsidiarity and devolution. The possibility of replacing Directives by Regulations (which are, under Article 189, of general application, binding in their entirety and, above all, directly applicable in all member states) has always appeared politically unacceptable. There is no suggestion that this situation will change in the 1996 IGC. In present circumstances, the Commission is faced with a mountain of implementing legislation in fifteen member states and in eleven official languages which has to be checked for conformity with EC Directives and then checked again to ensure that it is being correctly applied in practice. Quite simply, the task is impossible with the present level of resources.

The Commission is also in trouble over the administration of the EU's commercial policy. Apart from the negotiation and management of international agreements, the Commission is responsible for measures of commercial defence in the form of safeguard action and the imposition of anti-dumping and countervailing duties. Definitive action against imports is always taken by the Council, on a proposal from the Commission. The Commission itself may take time-limited provisional action. In both cases, the decisive preparatory work is conducted by the Commission's services.

Community law provides a number of procedural safeguards for industries and traders affected by commercial defence measures. Although consumers' interests should also be taken into account by the Community in reaching its decisions in the field of trade policy, in practice the interests of European producers have always greatly outweighed those of the European consumer. There is little evidence, particularly in a time of deep recession and unemployment, that this trend is changing. Although the sharp increase in the volume of commercial policy actions launched by the Commission between 1980 and 1990 has been accompanied by an increasing number of references to the Court, in practice the Commission retains a very wide (and substantially uncontrolled) discretion in its appreciation of the economic arguments for and against the adoption of measures of protection against imports.

In the conduct of anti-dumping or safeguard actions, the Commission naturally relies heavily on information supplied by the European complainant industry. It is true that the Commission will not decide on the formal opening of an investigation until it is satisfied that it has sufficient evidence that, for example, non-EC products are being dumped and are causing injury to European producers. On the other hand, the Commission's initial determination of dumping and injury is made without the traders or the non-EC industry concerned having the right to present their views. News that a complaint on dumping, or a request for safeguard action, has been submitted to the Commission circulates by rumour only. This in itself causes uncertainty and has an adverse effect on trade. Subsequently, the Commission's calculation of dumping margins and the assessment of injury to European producers involve calculations and methodology that have yet, despite specific provisions to this effect in the rules of procedure of the CFI, to be subjected to searching judicial review. Although the Court has been willing to admonish the Commission for failing to respect minimum procedural safeguards in dumping cases, it has generally been unwilling to review the substance of the Commission's economic findings.

One possible improvement would be to establish in Europe a specialised tribunal for the review of trade policy action by the EC. This would ensure a more effective separation of powers than currently exists. At present, the Commission drafts trade law and is simultaneously prosecutor, judge and enforcement agency. As far as democratic control of decision-making in trade policy is concerned, even under the Maastricht Treaty the Parliament is almost wholly excluded from the formulation, administration and execution of EC decisions on trade.

Apart from the decisions in the field of trade policy, there is no field of Union activity which impinges so directly upon private sector interests as that of competition policy, including state aids. EC law endows the Commission with the powers of legislator, watchdog, investigator, judge and enforcement authority. Although the ECJ (and, latterly, the CFI) have imposed disciplines on the Commission in its conduct of competition proceedings, the Commission continues to enjoy a measure of administrative discretion unparalleled in most national jurisdictions. It is true that the regulations provide a basis for quasi-judicial hearings by the Commission in anti-trust cases. This at least ensures that all interested parties have a right not only to submit their views in writing, but to be heard by the Commission before a decision is made. At the very earliest stage, the Commission may select the cases it wishes to deal with; subsequently it may decide whether to accept an informal settlement; and finally it decides on remedies or sanctions. The Commission's role is not only to decide which cases are well founded in law, but which cases are to be pursued as a matter of political preference.

The fact that the Commission's services in the field of trade, competition and infringements policy are over-burdened makes selectivity inevitable. The Commission acknowledges this situation, which is closely related to, though not entirely the cause of, its policy on the decentralisation of law enforcement. Whilst decentralisation may work to some extent in the field of infringements policy, it is less obvious that cases of unfair trade or competition can be so easily dealt with by national courts and tribunals.

Refusal by the Commission to open formal proceedings, particularly in anti-trust, state aids or trade policy matters, is very difficult to contest under EC law. Article 175 allows any natural or legal person to complain to the Court of Justice but the plaintiff has to demonstrate that it has been directly and individually concerned by the institution's failure to address an act to it, and this is never easy. In most cases, particularly where complainant enterprises are not well versed in EC law, the refusal of the Commission to take action in a particular case is effectively without judicial remedy.

The high-water mark of the Commission's administrative discretion lies in the informal settlement of cases. There is nothing inherently wrong with the principle of informal settlement. The accelerated enforcement of EC law which is possible through the Commission's periodic package negotiations with individual member states is to be welcomed. But in the case of unfair trade and competition matters there are frequently two or more parties with conflicting interests at stake in any given procedure. In these cases greater transparency is indispensable.

One of the most painful examples for companies of the Commission's discretion is in the imposition of fines in competition cases. Although subject to judicial review like any other Commission decision, the imposition of fines is based on an arcane and undisclosed methodology, and decisions on fines, as on many other important economic aspects of decisions in trade and competition policy, are taken at a relatively low level in the administration and inadequately reviewed at the political level. This underlines the need for an independent decision-making body (or bodies) in trade and competition matters, in which evidence can be heard and assessed in a transparently fair and even-handed manner. The situation in state aids investigations is even less favourable for companies than is the case with competition matters. Although, according to Article 93, all state aids are to be notified to the Commission for permission, the practice of member states is patchy. State aids investigations are frequently launched on the basis of a complaint from the private sector, but the complainant has no right to an oral hearing. Here again, the potential scope for administrative discretion tends to diminish transparency and the rule of law for companies, even if the scope for judicial review has been widened by a more flexible approach to admissibility in the CFI.

How the IGC can help

As far as the regulatory and decision-making powers of the institutions are concerned, therefore, particularly in fields such as law enforcement, trade and competition policy, urgent consideration must be given to the need to separate out the legislative, quasi-judicial and enforcement functions which are currently monopolised by the Commission, and to **the possibility of establishing tribunals in the fields of trade, state aids and competition policy**. Whatever else happens at the IGC, the European Commission must be given the proper resources to carry out its duties fairly, thoroughly and without undue delay.

Similar attention must be paid to increasing the resources and efficiency of the European Courts, and to safeguarding their independence. There are at present a corps of fifteen judges in each Court and nine advocates-general in the ECJ. Proposals for reform include allowing for dissenting minority opinions to be published, creating a number of regional CFIs, setting up an independent judicial appointments board and even — in order to check federal tendencies — establishing a supreme *Conseil d'Etat* made up of very grand jurists and statesmen. But the case for a radical change in the way the Courts work has not been well made. The principal problem is overload, faced with the prospect of enlargement. It would be irresponsible for this IGC not to address these issues, but premature for rigid decisions about the final size, shape or composition of the Courts. However, we would favour extending the term of office of the judges (from the current six to, say, ten years).

The important thing is that the IGC rises to the challenge of strengthening the Community's legal order to prepare for enlargement of the Union. For reasons of geographical size, linguistic and cultural differences and disparities in legal traditions and structures in an enlarged Union, it would already be a significant achievement to secure the full transposition and enforcement of the present acquis communautaire under the current system of judicial control. There are growing fears that the European Court of Human Rights is to be debilitated by the inclusion of some of the less reformed judges from ex-Communist Europe, and it is vital that the integrity of EC law is not similarly jeopardised upon enlargement of the Union.

The UK should cease to be hostile to the European Courts. Otherwise, the only serious prospect for strengthening the present legal order will be by recognising the inevitable need for a Europe of differentiated integration, involving different levels of commitment for different groups of states; and that will bring with it new risks for the rule of law.

There are four priority areas in which reforms are needed now, before enlargement.

These are:

1.   to extend the scope of the rule of law in the European Union, in particular to enlarge the jurisdiction of the ECJ to cover all the provisions of the third pillar and to strengthen its powers of judicial review of administrative action, especially in areas of decision-making which are close to the citizen;

2.   to widen access to justice at European level, especially for citizens and their associations: excessive formalism about who is a privileged litigant should be dropped;

3.   to review the administrative structure and resources of the Courts in order to cope effectively with its increased level of litigation brought about both by allowing the citizen direct access and by enlargement of the EU;

4.   to invest the European Union with full legal personality.

These reforms taken together will reinforce the rule of law and go some way to ensuring justice and fair play for the European citizen.

NOTES

1 European Commission, *Eurobarometer*, Brussels, 43, Autumn 1995, p. 8.

2 The main contributor to 'The European Citizen' is Andrew Duff, Director of the Federal Trust.

3 *Reflection Group's Report*, Brussels, 5 December 1995, para. 41.

4 UK White Paper, *A Partnership of Nations: the British Approach to the EU IGC 1996*, Cmnd 3181, London, HMSO, March 1996, para. 58.

5 77% of the British expect the EU to be fighting crime effectively in the year 2010, and 62% expect their children to be living and working anywhere in the EU; *Eurobarometer*, 43, op. cit., p. B-31; 72% of the British want today's EU to be waging war on drugs, and 44% want a common immigration policy, p. B-37.

6 Article 3b.

7 Article A.

8 These are reproduced in Andrew Duff (ed.), *Subsidiarity within the European Community*, London, Federal Trust, 1993, pp. 117-30.

9 See the Commission's *Report on Subsidiarity* to the Essen European Council, December 1994, COM(94) 533 final.

10 See for example, the Council's 1992 Convention on the Participation of Foreigners in Public Life at Local Level.

11 For a full analysis of the then 12 member states of the EU, see J.P. Gardner (ed.), *Hallmarks of Citizenship: a Green Paper*, London, The Institute for Citizenship Studies and the British Institute of International and Comparative Law, 1994.

12 See Anthony Lester QC, *Taking Human Rights Seriously*, 1994.

13 This on the grounds that an independent competent authority was not involved in the decision to exclude suspects or deport them (C175/94, *John Gallagher v. Secretary of State for the Home Department*).

14 See, for example, John Parry, *Citizen of the European Union*, London, European Movement, 1995; on 20 March 1989 the Parliament made a formal declaration of citizens' rights (De Gucht Report).

15 For a fuller analysis and discussion of CJHA, see the chapter by Malcolm Anderson, Monica den Boer and Gary Miller, 'European Citizenship and Cooperation in Justice and Home Affairs' in Andrew Duff, John Pinder and Roy Pryce (eds), *Maastricht and Beyond: Building the European Union*, London, Routledge for the Federal Trust, 1994; Michael Spencer, *States of Injustice: a Guide to Human Rights and Civil Liberties in the European Union*, London, Pluto Press, 1995; R. Bieber and J. Monar (eds), *Justice and Home Affairs in the European Union*, Brussels, European Interuniversity Press, 1995; and Alexis Pauly (ed.), *De Schengen à Maastricht: voie royale et course d'obstacles*, Maastricht, IEAP, 1996.

16 *Commission Report for the Reflection Group*, Brussels, May 1995, p. 51.

17 Article K.3.

18 *Reflection Group's Report*, op. cit., para. 46.

19 UK White Paper, op. cit., p. 22.

20 *Agence Europe*, 27-28 November 1995.

21 See Federal Trust Papers No. 3, *Building the Union: reform of the institutions*, London, Federal Trust, June 1995.

22 Interestingly, however, 67% of the British know about the European Parliament, 60% about the Court and only 42% about the Council; *Eurobarometer*, op. cit., pp. 38, 49-50.

23 *Agence Europe*, 25 November 1995.

24 This proposal is supported by many senior British judges. See, for example, Lord Slynn of Hadley in Alan Dashwood (ed.), *Reviewing Maastricht: Issues for the 1996 IGC*, London, Sweet and Maxwell for the Cambridge Centre for European Legal Studies, 1996, p. 68.

25 EC *Bulletin*, No. 7/8, 1995, pp. 8-9.

26 See *The Netherlands and Europe*, The Hague, Ministry of Foreign Affairs, 1995; and also the Benelux Memorandum on the IGC of 8 March 1996 which calls for 'sweeping reforms' of the third pillar, including powers of co-initiative for the Commission, jurisdiction of the ECJ, a role for the European Parliament and the incorporation of Schengen in the EU Treaty.

27 Ireland would want to join Schengen, but has a passport union with the UK; Denmark, Sweden and Finland have observer status, and discussions are continuing about Schengen and the Nordic passport union; Austria — and the European Commission — are also observers.

28 For example, Michel Barnier, European affairs minister, in the National Assembly on 13 March 1996 called for 'enhanced cooperation between some member states'.

29 This matter is also discussed in Federal Trust Papers No. 5, *Enlarging the Union*, London, Federal Trust, February 1996. The one exception to the general embargo on immigration is that Portugal has granted permission to enter the EU to 300,000 (mostly English-speaking) Macaoese — in marked contrast to the UK's treatment of British passport holders in Hong Kong.

30 See, for example, the article by Stephen Jakobi, 'Eurojustice in the balance' in *The Times*, 17 January 1995.

31 Official Journal C 158, 25 June 1986.

32 Article 118.

33 See Lord Cockfield, *The European Union: Creating the Single Market*, London, Wiley Chancery, 1994, p. 46.

34 For further development of this discussion, see Federal Trust Papers No. 2, *Towards the Single Currency*, London, Federal Trust, May 1995.

35 *Agence Europe*, 7 October 1995.

36 See *The 1996 IGC*, London, Justice, June 1995.

37 See *Building the Union*, op. cit., pp. 40-41.

38 Commission Opinion, *Reinforcing Political Union and Preparing for Enlargement*, March 1996, para. 39; European Parliament's Opinion on the convening of the IGC, Dury/Maij-Weggen Report, 13 March 1996, 4.9.

39 See Duff, *Subsidiarity*, op. cit., pp. 131-34.

40 See the Federal Trust Report, *Network Europe and the Information Society*, London, Federal Trust, July 1995.

41 See especially Article 126.

42 See a recent Federal Trust Report by Frances Morrell, *Continent Isolated: a Study of the European Dimension in the National Curriculum*, London, Federal Trust, 1996.

43 The main contributor to 'The European Legal Order at a Crossroads' is Alastair Sutton, Barrister.

44 For a more detailed discussion of these issues, see Kieran Bradley and Alastair Sutton, 'European Union and the Rule of Law' in Duff et al, *Maastricht and Beyond*, op. cit.

45 This term we owe to Alan Dashwood, now Professor of European Law at the University of Cambridge.

46 The expression European Courts refers both to the European Court of Justice and the Court of First Instance. Both submitted evidence to the Group of Reflection: Court of Justice, *Report on certain aspects of the implementation of the Treaty on European Union*, Luxembourg, May 1995; Court of First Instance, *Contribution with a view to the 1996 Intergovernmental Conference*, Luxembourg, 17 May 1995.

47 The Court added that 'the Community treaties established a new legal order for the benefit of which states have limited their sovereign rights, in ever wider fields, and the subjects of which comprise not only Member States but also nationals ... [T]he essential characteristics of the Community legal order which has thus been established are in particular its primacy over the law of the Member States and the direct effect of a whole series of provisions which are applicable to their nationals and to the member states themselves'.

48 The constitutional implications for Germany of the ratification of the Treaty of Maastricht are vividly illustrated in *Brunner v. The European Union Treaty*, 1994, CMLR 57. The judgment of the Federal Constitutional Court in this case provides a clear warning on the limits imposed by German constitutional law on the extent to which powers ceded to the EU may affect fundamental rights in Germany.

49 See A.G. Toth, 'A Legal Analysis of Subsidiarity' in David O'Keeffe and Patrick M. Twomey (eds), *Legal Issues of the Maastricht Treaty*, London, Wiley Chancery Law, 1994.

50 In other areas of constitutional significance, such as its unique power to initiate legislation on uniform electoral procedures, the Parliament has been unconscionably slow in discharging its duty.

51 For a full discussion of these issues, see Federal Trust Papers No. 4, *Security of the Union*, London, Federal Trust, October 1995.

52 Speech at the European Policy Forum, 12 May 1995.

53 *The Queen v. Secretary of Transport, ex parte Factortame Ltd*, Case C-48/93. The claims of several thousand BCCI depositors against the Bank of England, inter alia for failing to act in accordance with the Second Banking Directive, are still being heard by the High Court in England.